where i am

where i am

Written by
JESSE WARNER

where i am

First Edition

For you,

Because simply forgetting was never an option.

goya

(n) *Urdu, Pakistan* temporary moment
where fantasy feels real;
a story that feels like reality.

THE STORY

I don't wish to remember the end,
so I shall remember the story.

The sweetest thing she'll ever write.

I WROTE

Today I went to a museum.

When an artist sees beauty, he paints it.
When I found you, I wrote it.

CORNERS

She was a peculiar girl.

Who sat in the corner of libraries,
and flirted with the pages of books.

THE FIRST

She picked at her fingernails.
She was nervous.

He noticed and thought it was cute.
His eyes looked her up and down.

"So what do you like to do?" He asked.

Her eyes met his.

"I like to watch movies."

HISTORY

I will never forget the first time I met you,
and the burning desire to know what your bed
sheets looked like.

THE NIGHT CIRCUS

She fell in love on a Tuesday.

The days were sweaty and long, slowly melting off of the calendar's lazily hanging pages. The air was dense and her hair was cut short in an attempt to keep her cool. The flies never rested, and the farmer's crops hung their heads, exhausted from the days relentless heat. Relief only came with the promise of sundown.

The nights were a circus, as cooling air brought life to the village - rejuvenating the forest and waking each dragging sleepwalker. The woods were alive. And on the night that you kissed her, she saw each star a little brighter, felt each breeze a little closer, and heard each bug a little sharper.

As she walked home the moon guided her.
Her watch read 12:47AM.

It was Tuesday.

LOOSE LIPS

Some people become addicted to substances.
She became addicted to the way he said her name.

SPEECHLESS

There are so many beautiful words, but I can't find the right ones to say, she said.

That's okay, he replied. You are the most perfect kind of speechless.

SUNFLOWER

He was not something that was easily forgotten.
He was her sun, and for him she blossomed.

TWO THINGS

There are two things in this world every soul
wants to be: young and in love.

And darling, the stars have aligned - because we
are both.

WAVES

Sometimes I feel small, she said quietly, digging
her toes into the wet sand.

She hugged her knees, gazing out at the waves
that curled into themselves further than she
already had.

She was mesmerized, losing herself to the idea
of open water. Seemingly endless - but she
knew better.

I am a boat and you are the ocean, he whispered.
You are what keeps me afloat.

She turned her head, pressing her forehead
into his shoulder.

I won't let you sink.

ANSWER

It seemed almost instantaneous.

Just how quickly he turned from a question,
to the answer.

OCEANS KISS

The rhythm of their kiss,
   beating onto the shore,
   surrendered to bliss,
   wet clothes on the floor.

STOLEN

She was a smart girl,
who surrendered herself
to the love of another.

Her decisions made by
innocence and arrogance.

Her kisses taken on summer nights,
and heart stolen by
winter's morning.

CURVES

She fell in love with his hands,
and the way they made her back arch.

FOR HER

Her lips the sweetest symphony
his fingers ever played.

This song for her,
a lovers curse,
a bed now left unmade.

SOMEONE

There is a kiss,
    I've come to miss,
    from lips I have not met.

A step to take,
    but never took,
    a choice left to regret.

But in your arms,
    this place I know,
    and how could I forget.

The strangest thing,
    it is to miss,
    someone I've never met.

IMPACT

There was a moment of impact
when she realized she no longer
belonged to herself.

She was his.
And for him, she lost.

PARADOX

He was like flowers in her lungs: beautiful but lethal.

RICH

Their kisses were gold,
        but their love was cocaine.

RED

He changed like the leaves in autumn.
At first, hard to notice.
Until finally - he fell.

BOTTOM

I remember when I was falling.
Knowing I was going to hit the bottom.

But falling felt so good.

LICORICE

"Do we have any licorice?" she asked, groaning softly as she lifted the covers from her porcelain body.

He turned to the corner cupboard and pulled out a bag of red licorice. He could hear her toes on the hardwood floor, tiptoeing towards him.

Her pale body seemed almost translucent against the black curls that swept down her back. She reached out her hand, eager for her treat.

With a crooked grin he slowly placed the piece of licorice in her hand.

"You can repay me later," he said teasingly, reaching for her chin. She casually pulled back, smiling at his obvious disappointment.

"I don't think I could ever leave you," she said, sliding the piece of licorice into her mouth.

In that instant her smile faded and her expression became stoic. She was still. The only movement from her eyes that slowly crawled towards the floor.

He stared at her smiling, eyes confused while his mind wandered.

She bit down on the licorice and smiled, "but someday you'll leave me."

Her body lifted effortlessly onto her toes as she spun her body around and walked towards the bed. The red piece of licorice swaying at her side.

UNDONE

Of all the things she could undo,
he chose her,
while she chose you.

saudade

(n) *Portuguese* the feeling of intense longing for someone you love, but is now lost; a haunting desire for what is gone.

SLAM

On the day you left, every door closed.
I can still remember the sound.

Everything, and then nothing.

BROKE

She sat on the ground, staring at the decapitated sunflowers that slept in front of her.

She caressed the bright yellow petals, running her fingers over the freshly cut stems.

Slowly she tore off a petal, placing it in a small pile with the others she had plucked.

"It broke," she whispered, staring at the hedge cutters beside her.

WORDS

But that's the funny thing about words, she whispered.

They can't be unsaid.

THE BOX

She had a box.

And inside she hid all of the
things that made her
think of you.

She kept it closed and locked,
opening it only to try
and remember.

She would close her eyes and
reminisce on the days
she tried to forget.

Then she would close the box,
and put away all that
remained of you.

DAYDREAMS

She sat in the car like she had a million times before.
But this time was different.
This time she didn't want to be there.
She didn't want to be in the car.
She didn't want to be anywhere at all.

She drifted away, floating like a balloon into creamy
nothingness. She was numb.
There was no feeling, just being.
The words suddenly unsaid.
The fear pushed back into its corner.
The unthinkable was manifesting before her eyes.
The pieces of herself slowly being placed back into
working order.

* * * *

Lynn, he said coldly.

Her eyes flew open, pupils dilating rapidly.
She was back in the car. That fucking car.

Get out of the car Lynn.

APOTHECARY

Sleeping in this bed without
      you was too hard,
      but I tried.

I bought new sheets and kissed
      away anything
      you left beind.

Now I must take my pills,
      one at a time,
      and go to sleep.

Praying that when I close my
      eyes I forget that
      you still exist.

INK

There was supposed to be a point where she
paused and let go.
But she didn't.

Instead, she wrote down your name.

She wrote down your name nine hundred and
seventy four times.
She wrote your name until it lost its meaning.
She wrote it until it was no longer a name.

Just a time and a place.
A memory from an excellence.
Now so far away.

THE LAST LETTER

To be honest I see you in her, he wrote.

The sadness could not be replaced by pride,
nor arrogance.

It was like winning a game,
that's not meant to be won.

FORGET ME NOT

Forget me not,
      don't let me go.
      I'm too afraid,
      to finally know.

Know how it feels,
      to forget you not,
      for what you gave,
      is all I've got.

CYNICAL

She was no longer the same soul.
She had been tainted.

Her eyes dimly lit – complexion pale and lifeless.
Her heart was hallow and heavy, carrying
memories she no longer wished to remember.
She was sharp around every edge of her being,
cynical to the best of her abilities.

She was simply unsure whether she was too full,
or not full enough.

OUR WAR

Too far from my grasp,
and too much to ignore.

This love was too skinny,
left thin from the war.

Just how this war started;
your choice - my respect.

And no love could withstand,
that type of neglect.

ALL THAT IS LEFT

I don't understand why you write about it, he asked, trying to understand.

She considered this for a moment. Pausing to calculate her response.

I write because he took everything else. All I have left are these words - without these words, he doesn't exist.

FIRST OR LAST

I remember once when I was a child, I let a girl beat me at track and field, because I felt bad that I always came in first. My legs were long and hers were short, and it wasn't her fault she had that disadvantage. But when the race was over and she was handed my ribbon, I had nothing. My cheeks burned, and I wished I hadn't let her win that race.

When you left me for her, the same feeling burned into my cheeks. But this time it didn't make sense, because I had you first.

SAID

I said and I said- till all I had left,
was nothing to say.

THE SIMPLEST CHOICE

She remembers it loosely,
the first time it was said.

The way her head rested,
the sheets on the bed.

Just how her eyes watered,
the sound of his voice.

Of which to remember,
the simplest choice.

For what she remembers,
with absolute dread,

Is not the first time,
but the last
it was said.

TO JUDGE

I will never understand exactly what went wrong.
One moment you were there – and the next you
were gone.

But how could I judge what he thought belonged?

ALTERNATE UNIVERSE

I believe in an alternate universe, he said. *I think there is a place, just like this – only a little different.*

To this day, I wonder if there is such a universe.

A place where *is* never became *was.*

THE SIREN WITH STRAWBERRY CURLS

She was born to the sea, a creature of obvious
perfection. Strawberry curls rested on her breast as
she lay on the rocks, ocean's mist kissing her cheeks
as the hours dragged by. Most days she would sing,
her voice like gold, suspended in the open sea air.

Sprawled on her cliff one dry afternoon, a ship crept
along in the waters beside her. Delighted, she rolled
onto her stomach and began singing an irresistible
melody, gazing into the blue noon.

Her voice reached the ship and was heard by a
handsome sailor. Mesmerized by the sound - a melody
he had never heard - he leapt, plunging into the
ocean's grasp. He swam for the cliffs, desperately
following the enticing call.

As he reached the shore, he found the creature
waiting – her naked body seemed to sparkle, reflecting
the hanging sun. *I've been waiting forever,* she
whispered, kissing his ear, pulling at his wet collar.

Slowly she unbuttoned his shirt, bringing his face to hers, their lips first meeting. As he ran his hands down her back she continued to hum her siren call.

Soon the sailor had fulfilled all the siren needed from him; occupying the empty void she held, satisfying her hunger for intimacy. Thus, with one lingering kiss, she sighed, sending his body off the rocks, plummeting to his death below.

* * * * *

She watched the city skyline sparkle as she waited. Laying naked in his bed, she slowly rolled over, kissing his handsome nose to see if he had welcomed sleep. Satisfied, she gave him one last lingering kiss and casually rolled from his bed. Like a nude ballerina she walked on her toes, slipping back into her dress and out the studio's door.

Greeted by the cold night air, she lit a cigarette; her strawberry curls brushing her cheeks as she turned around the corner, not looking back.

THRENODY

He was a melody,
a song not known.

Her fingers did learn,
though notes not shown.

For he was her sun,
her stars,
her moon.

But every piano,
must lose its
tune.

THE WOMAN IN RED

Day after day the woman in red sat in her chair, gazing out her window. Arms relaxed on the windowsill, she would stare outside, transfixed by the day passing by in front of her youthful eyes.

With her hair short by her chin and her lips crimson red, she would spend her days lost to her sheltered delight. The days were routine and her life was secure, protected by the glass of her friendly window.

But eventually her days grew long and her window began to shrink before her eyes. Slowly, until one day, it was gone.

As she walked to her chair she patted the silk of her dress and sat down, starring at the plain white wall where her window used to be. Her heart sank and her eyes became heavy, filled with confusion and loss.

Day after day she would press her hands to the wall, waiting for her window to reappear - but it never did. Exhausted, she sat in her chair and closed her eyes, dreaming of the days she had spent in front of her tragically beautiful window.

As longing filled her heart, a cool breeze crept across her shoulder. She opened her eyes and turned around.

As she turned, she saw her living room; something she had rarely seen. The room was beautiful. White curtains danced in the breeze as sun slowly began to fill the room through every window.

The next morning the woman in red put on a blue dress. She walked down the stairs and took one last look at the empty white wall. With a thin smile, she opened every window and walked out the front door.

UNSAY

If words could be unspoken,
are there words you would unsay?

Unravel every little vowel
and let them float away.

My mind is curious,
thoughts unanswered;
these words I need to know.

And was my name,
each precious letter,
a hard one to let go.

DEVILS ADVOCATE

Of all the things I've had to learn,
     I never learned how
     to let you go.

We taught each other how to fall,
     without learning how
     to stand back up.

Looking back – we were reckless kids,
     who wanted nothing more
     than to be in love.

TUCKED AWAY

In the deepest corners of her mind,
she hides her favourite memories of you.

Tucked away, never to be found.

For when you are found,
is when you are missed.

And when you are missed,
she cannot be found.

COUNTING STARS

I close my eyes and let you in.
Counting stars I start to spin.

To see your face and feel your kiss.
All the things I've come to miss.

Eyes open wide from thoughts of you.
To miss you more is all I do.

So I close my eyes and let you in.
Counting stars I start to spin.

TO FORGET

The hardest battle,
> I've ever fought,
> was having you-
> till you were not.

PING AND PANG

You are like rain, the ping and the pang.
Once put me to sleep, now keeps me awake.

DAY AND NIGHT

From day to day,
And night to night,
The only thing,
That she can write,
Are thoughts of you,
And what she'd do,
To fall in love,
With someone new.

AWAY

Starting in fall,
    through spring to June,
    from eight to nine,
    and ten to noon.

In rain and snow,
    daylight and dew,
    she takes each step,
    away from you.

LITTLE WHITE LIE

I cannot help but remind myself that all that time,
you knew the truth. You allowed yourself to slowly
make terms with your decision, while I was kept in
the dark - sensing the instability of our delicate ship,
but desperately tugging at the sails anyhow. You
quietly become acquainted with your little white lie,
while I was building my entire life around it.

So when it was time for you to jump ship, you were
safe. Held securely by the life raft you spent those
months building, that I wasn't even able to see.

While I was left stranded on a ship that was sinking.
My life drowning in water; eyes frantically searching
for your hands to say goodbye.

GOODBYE

"I'll see you soon," he whispered, slowly letting her hand fall out of his.

"Don't say see you soon," she replied, "I know what this is – so just say goodbye."

"Goodbye then."

CHOOSING

With your choosing
    came my losing,
    from my faith
    my greatest loss.

So my choice
    became my
    moving.

Until your face
    I have
    forgot.

AN ANSWER

I'm not sure which is worse, but I beg for an answer.

Too scared to forget; too young to remember.

KETCHUP CHIPS

Remember when you were a kid, and you loved to eat a certain type of food? For me it was ketchup chips.

But now that you're older, and your tastes have changed, you suddenly don't like those foods as much anymore; perhaps you don't like them at all. Maybe you can't even stand the smell of them.
But oddly, you can remember the taste on the tip of your tongue. You can remember how much you used to love them.

That is how it feels to fall out of love.

One moment you're unwavering, and the next;
a ketchup chip.

LITTLE BITS

The most of you
  is far away,
  while little bits
  decide to stay.

To make their home
  within my veins.

And what I am,
  is what remains.

SOCKS

Do you know the feeling, when you're at the very
top of a roller coaster, just waiting for the drop?
Or when you watch a horror movie, and you
know something scary is about to happen?
How about when you leave the house and can't
remember if you left the oven on?

This is where you stay.

You are the horror every time I find one of your
socks in my closet two years later. You are the
skip in my heart when your smile enters my
unguarded mind. You are the crack in my voice
anytime your name is mentioned with hers.

AUTUMN LEAVES

I fear the seasons
    are backwards and wrong.

The leaves lose their colour,
    and birds lose their song.

But he would fall fast,
    while she would fall slow.

To wish you would stay,
    but watch as you go.

NOTHING

My eyes are shiny and palms are shaky
because the sky is too empty,
I can't find the moon

Like that night when I kissed you,
and you told me
you felt nothing

HELLO

I find myself wondering
where I'd be
if you never said *hello*.

Unsure I'd take it back,
but what I'd give
to know.

WHAT WAS

You were not a waste,
        but a point in time.

A nostalgic voice,
        to be left
        behind.

A winter night,
        when you dream
        of flowers.

You were mine,
        I was yours,
        we were ours.

BLIND

He was the most fortunate
and unfortunate
thing that ever came to be.

To hear the world
with eager eyes.

But left to never see.

BECAUSE

I wanted you to stay
(but not because I asked)

I'm trying to forget
(but not because you asked)

STAY

I never asked you to stay. Not once.

While my ears rang and my stomach turned, I
held my voice to keep it from shaking. The words
sat in my throat like acid, clawing at my lips,
screaming to be heard. But I held them tightly,
so close you'd never hear.

I whispered them to myself instead; both out of
fear and out of love. Never asking you to stay,
because I knew that you'd still go.

IF I CALLED

I find it strange, the things we remember
and the things we forget.
I can't help but wonder what you remember.

If I called, would you know it was me?

merkai

(v) *Greek* to do something with soul, creativity, or love; when you leave a piece of yourself in your work.

SHE WRITES

Fall in love with the words she writes.

Within each letter build your solace.

And every night,
let her sing you to sleep.

HEAVY AND BLUE

And every tear she cried was saved.
Held tight in a cloud, till it was heavy and blue.
So that one day she may dance.

Set free from the pain.
Knowing they were tears – and not just rain.

WITHIN THE WITHOUT

You must understand the importance of forgiveness.

Without forgiveness, you are within the without - wandering aimlessly amongst the unanswered questions and the years that have passed.

SCARS AND SPINES

When you asked to see my scars,
I had nothing to show.

But here they are now.

Locked in these words.
Embedded into its spine.

READ WHEN BROKEN

I know how you feel and I understand that it's hard.
You don't need to apologize or try to validate your
feelings to me. Your heart has been broken and that is
what matters. I do not care when and I do not care how;
all hearts bend differently but in the end they still break
the same. You have no control over how your soul will
try to cope, so I won't remind you of the facts because I
know that it won't help.

I'm not going to lie to you. I'm not going to tell you I
have the answers because honestly, I don't. It's likely
there are no answers for why you feel this way. People
are careless, even when they don't intend to be. I can't
tell you when the hurting will stop, or the day that you'll
feel better, but I can tell you that it's okay.

It's okay to feel this way. In fact, it's completely
reasonable. And although others won't understand your
suffering, that is no reason to think it's not valid. I will
not tell you how long it's been or remind you they've
moved on because that will not help you heal. But
eventually you will feel better. Eventually you will begin
to feel like yourself again and it will be refreshing. But
for now the world is yours, and you take every second
that you need.

SINK TO SWIM

An open heart is always elusive.
A precious pearl we must sink to find.

THE SEVERED ROAD

You and I walked a road
that was severed in two.

One destined for me
and the other for you.

While we each walk alone
on the road we call mine.

I still wait for the day
that our roads intertwine.

RACE

It's not a race – but my mind is running.

OBJECTS OF ATTACHMENT

Every person has a secret inventory of "things". I call them objects of attachment – things that refuse to be forgotten. Perhaps it's a place, a smell, a business card. Whatever it is, they refuse to go unnoticed. These objects are enchanted, taking us back to another time or another place, where things are very different from the way they are now. They make us nostalgic. Playing back memories like old black and white movies, flickering with shimmer and warmth.

They are hard to avoid – popping up when your mind is distracted. And regardless of what you threw away, or donated to charity, that is where you find yourself – starring at the game of Scrabble, wondering exactly how each piece used to fit.

While I know my inventory and have studied it well, I often wonder which objects I am attached to. And I find myself hoping that one day you find me, unexpectedly tucked away in the back of your closet, or a messy desk drawer – and remember exactly what we once were.

YEARS PASS

She began to exhibit reckless behaviour.

Like not brushing her hair,
and sleeping on what was once
his side of the bed.

INFINITE POSSIBILITIES

If all that there is – is all that there was,
     I shall consider myself blessed.

For I have seen every universe,
     held every star-
       never to be burned.

I have swam in every ocean,
     kissed every shore-
       never short of breath.

I have lived a thousand lives,
     in this finite life-
       never facing death.

So I consider myself blessed;
     that I lived within
       the infinite possibilities
       you created.

LOST AND FOUND

For all that is lost, must be found
someplace new.

And I have chosen here.

HARDENED

Sometimes I have a hard time feeling present.
As if I am plastic – living life through glossy
eyes and a hardened heart.

Perhaps I am more human when simply words
on a page.

FALLEN TREES

With empty rooms,
      and fallen trees,
      it's love that blooms,
      with you's and me's.

To fill this home,
      and make it new,
      to start alone,
      and then find you.

TRACKS

At night I lay in bed,
    listening to the distant sound
    of trains running their tracks.

But in a town as small as this,
    I know that my lullaby
    is your lullaby too.

LAVENDER

Sometimes this bed feels big
and I can't find sleep.
I miss you.

How you used to say I was your little bunny,
and hide lavender between my bed sheets.

GAMES

There is both beauty and pain in losing yourself to loving another. It is the most unmindful sacrifice we make as humans. Forgetting ourselves, to memorize another.

It is a strange misery however, to find yourself without. When we play, we may lose. But true suffering is with those who don't play at all.

WINE

You do not need happily ever after.

Just good books, good wine, and good conversation.

UNISON

I will hold my world
and you will hold yours

Until they collide,
they shall spin perfectly

Far apart,
but in unison

THE MOON

It's rather perplexing to know that you exist.
Living your life far away, but beside mine.
Seeing the same moon and watching the same
stars. Separated by thoughtless actions and the
time that inevitably passes.

I hope you look at the moon differently now.
Feeling as I do, looking and wondering if
you're seeing it too.

THESE WORDS

I have fallen in love with words.

And though they bring nothing back, they know
what you took. These words hold the secrets and
the stories that time could not heal. They carry
the weight that was too insufferable within these
fragile pages. These words hold the beauty that
once was, and the torment it became.

JENEPHER

You are the only soul I've ever met that loved the moon as much as I do.

Perhaps that's why she's been shining a little brighter.

"OKAY"

It's amazing. The way this world works. The way it kicks the shit out of you and demands that you stand up to take more the next day. It's scary how quickly things can change; whether we are ready for it or not. It's amazing how much a life can change in a matter of seconds.

But what's more amazing is how much a human is capable of feeling without exploding from all of the feel. What's unbelievable is the pain, both mental and physical, that a person can feel. I didn't even know such pain existed. And amazingly we survive. Not only do we survive, we're eventually "okay".

Eventually, after a long period of time, we're able to breath again. And not just a tiny inhale; a deep lung filling breath. A true breath, for the first time in what feels like your entire life.

So after all of it – the tears, the lies, the endless days of walking nightmares, everything is eventually and actually okay.

Now that's the most amazing thing.

MADNESS

I will never apologize for my madness.
A life with sanity is absent of love.

GRATEFUL

Why are you crying.

*Because you're hurting so badly and there's nothing I can do.
I'm sorry that I can't make this all go away.*

* * * * *

It wasn't your heart that broke. It was mine.
But all these years later I remember it was you that cried.
Because I couldn't.
And for that I am eternally grateful.

DIRECTION

I'm trying not to question things anymore.
It has kept me in the same place for far too long.

I would rather walk with today's sense of
direction than yesterday's anyhow.

DEAR FRIEND

There is no need to apologize.

It was simply a try. A second try, a third, and now
the end. The promise of change was fleeting and
his words were gentle, but now they are far away.
Each day they grow further and somehow it only
starts to hurt more.

As your heart splits and your eyes fill, mine will
too. While I sit on my bed and you lay on the
floor my heart will break a thousand times with
yours. You cannot imagine how much I hate that
I could say I told you so. So I won't.

And while every piece of your being feels
betrayed and lost, know that I offer your heart a
home. There will always be a bed with your name
on it and a hug when you need it. And even
though he is gone, I am here; with bottles of wine
and promises that I promise won't break.

SIMPLICITY

Last night I had the overwhelming urge to look at
the sky. As I stood on that gravel road, face tilted
upward, I opened my eyes.
A river of shining freckles lay scattered across the
midnight ceiling. Each star had its place, perfectly
unorganized, strewn across the night sky.

While I understand these stars have long died, and
all I see are their final thoughts, I cannot help but
admire the overwhelming simplicity.

And strangely I'm left inspired, that something so
long gone can still be so bright; left to guide the
wandering and find the lost.

REASON

Why did no one consider that she was alone
for a reason.

In her seclusion she was beautiful;
so breathtaking it could bring you to tears.

BACKWARDS

I never thought I'd look at you this way.

I never thought my bones would ache or my
hands would shake the way they do. Just the
mention of your name could send me into a dark
room with a locked door and I never thought I'd
have to scream to find a way out.

But the earth was so damn tired of spinning with
such predictability that it started to spin
backwards. And slowly I began to look at you
whole again. Suddenly and without warning I was
able to see you as you were, all those years ago,
when the future was unthinkably different from
the way it is now.

The universe may be unkind. But in that
moment, spinning backwards, it was kind to me.

THE GOOD LIE

But when she asks about me, because she will ask, tell her a lie. Tell her a lie that is sweeter than honey and softer than silk. Give her the kindest reassurance so that she may continue to sleep softly, because lately she has tossed and turned. When you whispered my name that night as you slept, you shook the gentle seas within her. And when the waves begin to swallow her whole, she will beg for an answer.

I don't want you to feel remorse. Though you knew this day would come, you could not possibly prepare yourself for the melody of her plea and absence of all reason. She has no idea that within her simple request she will shake the gentle seas within you as well.

Ride these waves with compassion. Remember that she has no idea the way our lips danced or the promises that sang us to sleep. The secrets we held and the demons we shared. She doesn't care to hear our stories and she doesn't need to know how much I loved your mother. Don't tell her we grew up together, best friends who fought our fears, hand in hand like nothing mattered.

And forget the place where we promised each other we would never give up. But above all, you should fail to mention that I was the first girl who truly held your heart.

Carry yourself with your calm demeanour and promise that the world is hers. And when you tell her she is beautiful, try not to remember that you said the same to me as well. Give her every reassurance that she needs, because trust me darling; she needs it far more than I. Her insecurity only proves that she loves you. Perhaps just as much as I did.

So when she asks about me, tell her not to worry. Tell her the stars shine for her and for her alone. Tell her she is everything, and that my name is simply an echo from a time that holds little significance to you now.

For now she holds your heart. And when you whisper my name in your sleep once again, at least this time she will have her answer.

LIVE

We may live – or endure.
The choice is ours and we needn't ask for permission.

IN THE NEXT

Though I likely won't forget,
it is time to move on.

To live this life as it is,
and find you in the next.

HOME

And regardless of the losses,
the heartaches, and the fails.

My final words to you are,
thank you.

These words have made me human.
These words have brought me home.

INDEX

Section Three: Merkai

Printed in July 2021
by Rotomail Italia S.p.A., Vignate (MI) - Italy